Virgin MoDERN iCoNS

THE KINKS

Acknowledgements

With very grateful thanks to Philip Dodd, Morse Modaberi,
Helen Johnson and to Michael Heatley,
Northdown Publishing and the staff of the National Sound
Archive for their help in the research of this book.

Colin Shearman has been a regular contributor to *The Guardian*
arts page since the 1980s, as well as working for *Time Out* as a
TV writer. He has been writing for *Q* magazine since its very first
issue, and specialises in rock music from the 1960s.

First published in 1997 by
Virgin Publishing Ltd
332 Ladbroke Grove
London W10 5AH.

Modern Icons series conceived and developed
for and with Virgin Publishing Ltd by Flame Tree Publishing,
a part of The Foundry Creative Media Company Limited,
The Long House, Antrobus Road, Chiswick, London W4 5HY.

Modern Icons series © Virgin Publishing Ltd 1997
Text © Flame Tree Publishing.

ISBN 1 85227 678 9

A catalogue record for this book is available from the British Library.

Virgin MoDERN iCoNS

THE KINKS

Introduction by Colin Shearman

CONTENTS

CONTENTS

INTRODUCTION

Britain was a strange place in 1964. Cultural barriers had been falling as the 'angry young men' movement swept through literature and the theatre, and disaffected young musicians were also starting to express their anger and frustration at how things were. If you'd asked any of them exactly what they were rebelling against, they'd probably have mimicked Marlon Brando's famous line from The Wild One – "What you got?" – but there was definitely a new anti-authoritarian attitude making its presence felt in the early R&B-based work of The Kinks, The Rolling Stones and The Who.

The Kinks's 'You Really Got Me', released in August 1964, just as Merseybeat was losing its chirpy charm, was one of the first records to really pick up on this aggression and refusal to kow-tow to authority. It may have taken The Who to articulate the idea fully a year later in songs like 'My Generation', but it was certainly flexing its muscles in the raw, heavy guitar riffs of the Kinks's first hit and the follow up 'All Day And All Of The Night'.

Many accounts of the group's early days often slot them in as a Sixties art school band because of songwriter/lead-singer Ray Davies's student background, but his younger brother, Dave, who actually formed the group was more responsible, both musically and visually, for their early success.

His wild image and stage act, wearing outrageous clothes and playing frenzied guitar solos on his knees, made The Kinks one of the first pop groups with attitude. Lead guitarist Dave also invented the heavily distorted guitar sound which charged their early records with so much energy. Via their influence on The Who, he established power chord riffs as part of rock's basic language, paving the way for heavy metal and, eventually, punk.

In fact, the legendary resentment and on-and-off stage fighting between the two brothers is at least partly down to the fact that, as with Oasis, an elder song-writing sibling joined up at a later stage and eventually took over his younger brother's group. As late as 1989, Ray was nursing a crunched knuckle where he'd hit a wall rather than his younger brother's head in a studio argument. And like Oasis, The Kinks's long-running success is also partly due to the competitive, creative tension between the brothers.

Given the group's early image, Ray Davies was always quite happy in many of their initial hits to come across as some kind of passive sexual object, in songs like 'You Really Got Me', 'Set Me Free' and 'Tired Of Waiting For You'. So it was no surprise that once he'd established himself, he got down to the serious business of being the bloke sitting in the corner who just watches the world go by: Terry and Julie walking over Waterloo bridge in 'Waterloo Sunset' or the 'Dedicated Follower Of Fashion' pulling up his frilly nylon panties in Carnaby Street. The first signs of this change came with the December 1965 EP 'Kwyet Kinks' in which, on tracks like 'A Well Respected Man' and 'Such A Shame', he began to adopt a more lyrical, very English style of writing which embraced satire, social comment and nostalgia, frequently in a melancholy way.

He also developed a knack for telling little stories about slightly odd or engaging characters that set new standards in pop writing. 'Dandy', for instance, satirises an ageing philanderer, 'Situation Vacant' introduces a domineering mother-in-law while 'David Watts' – later covered by The Jam and apparently stealing the name of a real-life concert promoter who tried to seduce Dave Davies while on tour – is a wonderful study of adolescent hero-worship. Sixties rivals like Paul McCartney and Pete Townshend often told stories in their songs too but, with odd exceptions such as 'Eleanor Rigby', their characters were frequently just ciphers to move the three-minute plot along. They rarely managed to bring them to life as Davies did.

Ray and Dave were brought up in the 1950s in Muswell Hill, North London, in the run-down part of an otherwise fairly middle-class area. Growing up amid such social inequalities may well account for

how obsessed Ray was in his songs with the English class system. In 1966, while others were falling for the myth of swinging London as a classless society where cockney pop stars and photographers could rub shoulders with minor aristocracy, Davies was describing the death of the post-war dream in two highly successful singles viewed from either side of the class barrier: the dispossessed and nearly bankrupt aristocrat dreaming of tax exile in 'Sunny Afternoon', followed a few months later by the demoralised working-class family trying to make ends meet on 'Dead End Street'.

Despite being dismissed by many people, including DJ Tony Blackburn, as much too dreary a subject for pop music, 'Dead End Street' nonetheless became a Top Five hit. Its theme of ordinary people struggling in the modern world cropped up time and again in Davies's work over the next few years: especially in his concept albums 'Arthur (Or The Decline And Fall Of The British Empire)' and 'Muswell Hillbillies'. This kind of detailed social observation, reflecting the preoccupations of working-class novelists like Allan Sillitoe and David

Storey but quite new in British pop music, helped break down the barriers between high and low art so common at the time. Davies's concern for the failed aspirations of ordinary people also made The Kinks one of the few Sixties groups acceptable to punk and new wave bands in the Seventies, influencing in particular The Jam's many songs about urban angst. What is 'A Town Called Malice' if not 'Dead End Street' re-written from a more strident, political viewpoint?

Also breaking new ground for the time in its intended mix of beat music and serious drama was 'Arthur (Or The Decline And Fall Of The British Empire)'. Originally planned as a TV play for Granada Television with a script by respected writer Julian

Mitchell, the play was eventually axed for financial reasons and the 'soundtrack' album appeared on its own. The loosely connected songs look back over the life of an ageing World War I veteran, Arthur Morgan, on the day his son and daughter-in-law emigrate to Australia. Tracks such as 'Shangri-La', 'Yes Sir, No Sir' and the title track are bitter complaints about the way ordinary people who'd made heroic sacrifices in both world wars had been pushed around or sold down the river ever since. 'Muswell Hillbillies', recorded two years later and inspired by the compulsory re-housing of the Davies brothers' elderly grandmother in an anonymous council flat, describes the way traditional working-class communities – and the values they represented – were being mindlessly destroyed by Sixties redevelopment.

Davies's retreat into nostalgia on these two concept albums and their predecessor, '(The Kinks Are) The Village Green Preservation Society' (1968) is often put down to his own sense of rootlessness and dismay at modern life. Admittedly, he's always had a tendency to nostalgia, as in the much-covered B side 'Where Have All The Good Times Gone?', but there's more to it than that.

At the height of the Kinks's fame in the Sixties, there was a strong feeling – based on the encroachment of American popular culture and a public debate about whether or not Britain should join the Common Market – that England and the English identity were

being swallowed up. It was an affection for all things British and a way of life that was disappearing which led Davies, by his own account, to present English traditions in his work and write about specifically English subject matter, even deliberately trying to sing in an English voice (from the cheeky-chappie music hall tradition of 'Autumn Almanac' to the upper-class accent in 'Sunny Afternoon') rather than the transatlantic drawl offered by most pop stars of the time.

In this respect, an interesting comparison can be made with those other great satirists of the sixties, Private Eye magazine. Both Private Eye's sneers at anything modern and Davies's respect for the old ways of life were equally fuelled by the gradual disappearance of the England they loved. It all comes down to the old cliché, 'If You Didn't Laugh, You'd Have To Cry'. Where the mainly public school, Oxbridge-educated *Private Eye* crowd chose to laugh, often cruelly, Davies, the secondary modern boy from Muswell Hill, chose to cry.

That's not to deny the wit and humour in his songs but even his most comic material still has a sense of loneliness behind it. And it's here, perhaps – in songs aching with loss such as 'Days', 'Wonderboy' and 'Celluloid Heroes' – that he's had his greatest influence. Effectively, these songs argued, by their very existence, that it was all right for men to show their feelings, to admit to being confused, unhappy and lonely. This debate about men's emotional behaviour is still very much going on today but in the Sixties, boys were still brought up as a matter of course to hide their feelings; and Davies, working in a popular, influential mass medium, was one of the first to break

down this stiff upper lip attitude. His own favourite self-composition may be 'I'm Not Like Everybody Else', but one of the Kinks's big attractions is that his best lyrics articulate the loneliness and vulnerability we all feel at times.

This particular aspect of Davies's work also initiated a highly eccentric, English strain of pop music, from the ironic self-doubt of so many Smiths recordings to Squeeze's three-minute

dramas about English low life, XTC's quirky lyrics and the vaudeville tones of Blur's songs about humdrum lives. 'Ernold Same' on Blur's 'The Great Escape' was originally entitled 'Dear Ray' as a tribute to the chief Kink, while 'Country House' and 'Charmless Man' on the same album were obviously partly inspired by the Kinks's own 'House In The Country' and 'A Well Respected Man'.

However, it wasn't just musically that the group influenced the record industry. When Ray Davies married his first wife, Rasa, he couldn't even afford to buy a house to live in, although he'd written over half a dozen hit records. Due to the group's inexperienced management at the time, he'd been encouraged to sign a particularly unfair publishing deal when starting out and so spent the next four years fighting all the way to the Court Of Appeal to have the contract annulled. Eventually winning his case proved another watershed for the music business.

These events provided material for the group's highly satirical exposé of the record industry, the oddly named album 'Part 1: Lola Versus Powerman And The Money-Go-Round', with its music-hall ukuleles poking fun at music publishers in Denmark Street alongside Davies's own amused resignation as his managers and agent divide up his royalties amongst themselves on 'The Money-Go-Round'. More importantly, the other title track, 'Lola', with its camp sexual ambiguities and word-play started the Kinks's big break through in America – eventually resulting in the huge US success of late Seventies albums like 'Sleepwalker' and 'Low Budget' whose crowd-pleasing

heavy guitar work brought Dave Davies back much more to the fore.

During the Seventies and Eighties, though, Ray's heart was only really in attempts to merge theatrical and musical events. He enjoyed some success here in his collaborations with the British playwright, Barrie Keeffe, and his own musical TV play, *Starmaker*, but his mid-Seventies *Preservation* stage shows – combining film, theatre and music – were critically panned.

Other ventures like his 1984 Channel 4 screenplay *Return To Waterloo* were generally considered too unfocused written from too personal a viewpoint. To date, he still hasn't written the great rock'n'roll stage musical so long expected of him. In retrospect, it seems his role was to bring theatrical and literary qualities to pop music rather than the other way round.

Since The Kinks have spent so much of their career under the possibly more glamorous shadow of The Beatles and The

Stones, many people often under-estimate just how influential they've been. At the same time, any assessment of their career must inevitably conclude that they've never really fulfilled their true potential – and one suspects the reason for this lies firmly in Ray Davies's own ambivalence towards fame and fortune. In 'Sitting In My Hotel', the hauntingly sad track from the 1972 album 'Everyone's In Showbiz,

Everyone's A Star', he debates the pressures of fame, while 'Celluloid Heroes' presents the many movie stars whose handprints are encased in cement outside Mann's Chinese Theatre on Hollywood Boulevard as ordinary, frail people – and all the better for that.

Along with John Lennon's post-Beatle work, Davies has been at the forefront in blowing the whistle on fame in this way, but, unlike Lennon, this uncertainty has filtered through in a negative way into the group's real life and career: the missed opportunities, the stage fights, the endless problems with promoters and agents. It's pointless to speculate, though, about what might have happened if things had been different. This outer turmoil in the group obviously to some extent reflects the inner turmoil in both brothers' souls and, without that, we wouldn't now be celebrating one of the most interestingly eccentric English groups or one of the greatest and most meaningful collections of rock songs ever written.

Colin Shearman

KITH AND KINK

Thirty years before Noel and Liam Gallagher, the brothers Ray and Dave Davies had already brought sibling camaraderie and rivalry to the charts.

Because we're brothers, Ray and I are a lot closer than most, but we're opposed in a lot of ways.
Dave Davies, 1978

I tried to stab Dave last month. We were having something to eat after a gig, and he took one of my chips. Got him right under the ribs. It was horrible.
Ray Davies, *Crawdaddy* magazine, 1976

Were Dave and Ray Davies related?, asked *Melody Maker* in 1964
Yeah. We're sisters.
Ray Davies

Dave was the practical one, Ray the one who couldn't get things together. Dave was the tearaway, the natural extrovert, Ray the loner, who felt totally insecure on stage. It took him a long time to relax in performance.

I pity anybody who relies on me for their welfare. Really I've got no idea. Sometimes I wonder how I've kept the band together.

Ray Davies

Circus: You're so extroverted on stage and so shy off stage.

Ray: I thought about that a lot. I'm not always shy. Maybe I'm relaxed on stage more, because I enjoy it.

Circus magazine, 1974

The other 'brothers' in the original Kinks were drummer Mick Avory and bassist Pete Quaife.

[Mick] had really short hair – he was a bit of a rocker, his hair greased back and all. He hadn't met us before so he decided to have his hair cut and put on a suit to create the right impression, and when he got there we're sitting around in jeans and scarves and long hair and he thought to himself 'God, what did I do?'. But he came along at just the right time.

Dave Davies

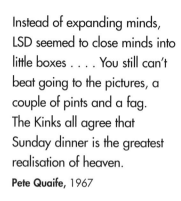

Instead of expanding minds, LSD seemed to close minds into little boxes . . . . You still can't beat going to the pictures, a couple of pints and a fag. The Kinks all agree that Sunday dinner is the greatest realisation of heaven.
Pete Quaife, 1967

Pete Quaife was the true amateur. He's not a great music lover, but Pete did it because he enjoyed life. And he was my friend. The day we stopped communicating onstage was a good time to stop.
Ray Davies, *NME,* 1977

The band was created from an R&B outfit called The Ravens, and developed by their first managers Robert Wace and Grenville Collins, agent Arthur Howes and fixer Larry Page.

We were really an instrumental based group. I was really into The Ventures, and I remember saying it'd be great one day, Dave, if we could have a group like The Ventures with vocals on top. The Ventures were sort of dry, and they had that chunky guitar: really ahead of its time. I did a third of the vocals, and there was no harmonies. And I really wasn't into songwriting at all.

Ray Davies, *Melody Maker*

KINKY, KINKY

· ·

The change of name from The Ravens to
The Kinks was the decision of one of the
management entourage – Robert Wace or
Larry Page, depending on the version.
Whatever, it suited the mood of the times.

Now Beat Goes Kinky!
We're going back to gimmicks.
At the moment, long hair is old hat.
It's the name game. This week we turn to The
Kinks. They claim their name was suggested by
some of their followers, on account of the kinky
hats they wear on stage – the fashionable fat
caps seen around – and their stylish boots.
Melody Maker, 1964

It's like a catch phrase, you see. You
hear people saying 'That's a bit kinky'
referring to the wild hats we wear, so
that's how the name came up.
Ray Davies, 1964

The band had an early reputation for outrageous clothes. Their relationship with Carnaby Street would later be gently lampooned by Ray Davies in 'Dedicated Follower Of Fashion'.

There were a lot of plastic boots and stuff like that around, and I used to wear a sort of plastic coat with high, cavalier type boots that I'd gotten from a friend of mine who used to work for a theatrical costume place. There were a lot of shops around using the word 'kinky' and it got associated with the clothes we wore.

Dave Davies, *Trouser Press,* 1978

Our manager said we needed really outrageous stage suits so we spent all our money getting John Stephen of Carnaby Street to make these awful itchy Thames green suits. The trousers were really tight with leather straps so our Cuban heels could get through, and matching straps on the sleeves and collars. We wore them with leather caps and looked like prats.

Ray Davies, 1994

*Partly from their flamboyant clothes –
pink hunting jackets and frills were
the norm – the Kinks became something
of a gay icon, especially Dave.*

Not only did they invent heavy metal,
but it just might have been The Kinks
who invented glam rock, way back in
the '60s, when Ray would twitch his
bum and wave a languorous finger over
his head, pouting and camping.
Phil McNeill, *NME,* 1974

It created a bit of interest in the beginning,
being invited to all these gay parties.
Dave Davies, 1978

After we put out 'Dedicated Follower Of
Fashion' in 1966 . . . my agent came up to
me and said, 'Ray – are you *queer*?'. I
didn't know I was writing that kind of song.
Ray Davies, *Crawdaddy,* 1976

BROTHER DAVE

Guitarist Dave was the driving force behind the raunchy Kinks sound on early singles like 'You Really Got Me' and 'All Day And All Of The Night'.

I got fed up with that tinny sort of guitar sound that you'd get. Just out of boredom one day I ripped up the speakers of this little amp I had – it was like ten watts – and I played through it. The noise that came out was so amazing that I used to link it up with the regular Vox amplifiers. I just put a lot of bass on the little amp and it started to really fart, it was great. All the engineers that worked on our sessions probably hate me from a technical standpoint.

Dave Davies, *Trouser Press, 1978*

*His guitar technique had evolved
out of necessity. Ray later said
that they couldn't copy Buddy
Guy like Page or Clapton so they
simply had to adapt the sound.*

That's why we were original.
Ray Davies, *Mojo, 1995*

Playing gives a great sense of
self-expression, the energy you
create by playing. I used to get
mad, and I suppose I'm sort of
schizophrenic at heart as well.
Dave Davies, 1978

Dave's solo had nothing to do
with music. When the solo came I
just stared at him. I think he did it
out of fear more than anything.
Ray Davies, on Dave's solo on 'You Really
Got Me', *NME, 1977*

Though Dave downplayed his own technical ability, his influence was strong, but often lost in the shining light of brother Ray's songwriting skills.

I never was a very good guitarist – and I'm still not. So I used to experiment with sounds. Musically, it was probably awful, but it meant a lot to me.
Dave Davies

Instant Kinks they call us! When we're in a studio, I have nothing worked out. Till the red light goes on, I don't really know what I'm going to play.
Dave Davies, *Melody Maker,* 1965

I don't think he's had the credit he deserves.
Ray Davies, on Dave, *Dark Star,* 1979

41

BROTHER RAY

Despite Dave's input, Ray was clearly the leader of The Kinks.
As well as his songwriting, he contributed his distinctive voice
to the musical mix, an English accent clearly different from
the prevailing nasal Merseybeat or affected cockney.

To most intents and purposes, Ray Davies *is* The Kinks.
NME, 1977

The prevailing spirit of The Kinks is Master Wizard Warlock
Raymond Douglas Davies. Davies is the Kinks's spokesman,
songwriter, rhythm guitarist and vocalist. But, even as the star
focal point he is totally enmeshed in the kinky fiber of his band.
Circus magazine, 1974

Probably my signature is my voice,
that's how you suss out who it is.
Ray Davies

Tiny little voice coming through those heavy chords.
Making Music, 1989

A vocalist who was able to adopt roles in his singing, Ray's songwriting was – and is – full of unforgettable characters, and a wistful, wry humour.

I was standing at a bar the other day and a guy came up to me, and said, 'Ray, I like your songs, you know I think you're a very under-rated songwriter, a poet really' . . . . So I hit him over the head with a beer bottle.
Ray Davies, 1972

All the while Ray's laughing; he's laughing at me, laughing at you, but more than anything else he's laughing at himself.
Journalist, **Karen Hughes,** *Melody Maker*

I hate people saying 'Oh, here is a new Kinks record, it'll be a great tongue in the cheek record' because a lot of the time I'm trying to be deadly serious'
Ray Davies,
Zigzag, 1969

*Ray Davies is a
songwriter's songwriter - the
consummate craftsman.*

You can say everything in three
minutes and I will always
subscribe to that. I hope it will
never die, it's a lovely art form.
Ray Davies, *Mojo,* 1995

More than any strictly musical
quality, the source of the group's
longevity and vitality is this
sensibility – Ray's kinks, if you will.
Ken Emerson, *Rolling Stone*

When I was at art school as a
student, what I got out of it was
colour, expression. Now I find you
turn out a bad song for the same
reason you turn out a bad painting
– insincerity. If you are sincere –
if you do what *you* want – you
can't turn out a bad thing.
Ray Davies, *Melody Maker,* 1964

46

*After the publication of his autobiography X-Ray,
and The Kinks's induction into the Rock and Roll
Hall of Fame, Ray has taken on, possibly against
his own instincts, the mantle of an elder statesman.*

We have never been a fashion band.
People like us because we're not out to trick them.

Ray Davies, *19 magazine,* 1982

I don't put people down for taking my style and finding
something of their own, but I don't think Tom Robinson has

found anything original
yet. He's only saying
things that I said on
Preservation. I don't think
there's anything original
there. *I* am
an original.

Ray Davies, 1976

DEAR OLD BLIGHTY

● ●

The Kinks's songs are frequently infused with views and memories of an England remembered and an England experienced.

Just going abroad and seeing different people has made me feel English because unless you experience other things you don't know who you are.

Ray Davies, *Dark Star,* 1979

A vanishing, romanticized world of village greens, pubs and public schools is the elegiac source of Ray's sometimes fearsome defense of traditional values; he contrasts the faded charms of an ended Empire to the dole queues and dark skies of today's collapsed England, and he's alternately bitter and paralyzed with pathos.
Rolling Stones Album Guide

My Englishness doesn't leave me, does it? The things that appeal to me and inspire me are still English things.
Ray Davies, *19 magazine,* 1982

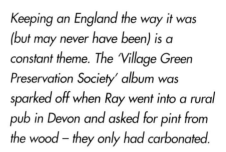

Keeping an England the way it was (but may never have been) is a constant theme. The 'Village Green Preservation Society' album was sparked off when Ray went into a rural pub in Devon and asked for pint from the wood – they only had carbonated.

I notice the difference. Some wouldn't. But it doesn't get you in the legs any more . . . . I get the feeling that soon everybody in Britain will be talking with the same accent.
Ray Davies, *Rolling Stone,* 1974

Like Kevin Ayers, Bryan Ferry, Syd Barrett and precious few other people working in pop/rock music, Ray Davies is human – and English. He looks English, he sounds English and thinks English. Who else but Ray Davies would sing about Waterloo Station and Muswell Hill and village greens.
Melody Maker, 1974

The chart success of 'Sunny Afternoon' coincided with England's victory in the 1966 World Cup, and the synchronicity was perfect.

Sunny Afternoon. I remember the record coming out and I walked into a British Legion or a pub. All these people, old soldiers and things, singing it. I was 23 years old. I said 'Wow, all these old people really like it.' And this old guy came up and said 'You young guys . . . this is the sort of music we can relate to!'

Ray Davies, *Mojo,* 1995

Strange newly composed by leader Ray Davies in a slightly rawer Lovin' Spoonful style. Starts with a long bass run down which reminds you of the Beatles's 'Michelle' mixed with Nancy Sinatra's 'Boots'. Ray takes the lead vocal in a ridiculously lazy slurred style . . . .Some might find the length and repetitiveness of this disc a bit too much, but its lazy atmosphere should certainly catch on with summer on the way.

Melody Maker, June 1966

I had to come off the road. I was ill. I cracked up considerably. I was a zombie. I just stayed in a room in darkness at the middle of the day, and I would eat salads and go to bed early.

Ray Davies on his state of mind when writing 'Sunny Afternoon'

'Waterloo Sunset' was released in May 1967, and mixed a quintessentially British scene with typical Davies melancholia. Apparently the song was originally meant to be 'Liverpool Sunset', but Ray thought it was too close to the Liverpudlian feel of The Beatles's 'Penny Lane' from early that year.

I drew on images from the subconscious and things that worked with the melody, and, in that case, finishing the song and the record was like finishing a painting. It's a song about a moment in time but it's also a kind of eternal thing, and that's why people like it. The underlying mood is very sad. The world will never be the same again and I'm a little bit scared but I take consolation in seeing the sunset and knowing there will be another sunset and there will be sunsets long after I'm dead.
Ray Davies, *Mojo,* 1995

'Brooklyn' is a simple impressionistic piece doing for New York what Ray Davies's 'Waterloo Sunset' did for London, with similar touches of the urban poetic.
Stephen Barnard, *Let It Rock* magazine, 1974,
on Steely Dan's 'Brooklyn (Owes The Charmer Under Me)'

Despite Ray's English obsessions, his views about America – in the Seventies the strongest market for The Kinks – were somewhat mixed.

I hope England doesn't change. I'm writing a song now called 'You Ain't What You Used To Be' which expresses what I feel. I hope we don't get swallowed up by America and Europe.

Ray Davies, 1966

'Waterloo Sunset' came out of London and 'Celluloid Heroes' came out of Hollywood and they're both the same as far as I'm concerned. The difference is you can't be in two places at once.

Ray Davies, 1974

People think the world revolved around London and it doesn't. I do dislike this thing prevalent now of overdoing the English accents. That's a bit too cute. I'm really proud of being English. But my musical influences for the most part were American.

Ray Davies, 1995

SLICES OF LIFE

*Down-to-earth, ordinary
people, everyday situations.
The essentials of Ray
Davies's songwriter's palette
have a universal appeal.*

Basically, everybody is a
poor sod. Those people
only stay there because
they're afraid to get out.
Ray Davies, *Zigzag,* 1969

I think his poetry is fantastically
good. Because I really enjoy his
symbols. Very simple. Very
straightforward, using the
language that everybody knows.
Jefferson Airplane/Starship's
Marty Balin

It seems that when a thing is 'down-to-earth' and factual people always try to stamp it out, but eventually it becomes the established thing. I hope eventually to become sufficiently capable of expressing people's everyday moods, thoughts and emotions in music. Maybe we should be called the Francis Bacons of pop music!

Ray Davies,
Melody Maker, 1964

The singles 'A Well-Respected Man', and particularly 'Dedicated Follower', were the first releases that marked a change of direction from the early hits to vignettes of characters like Pink Floyd's 'Arnold Layne' and 'See Emily Play' and the London life captured in the Small Faces's 'Lazy Sunday'.

This doesn't sound like the same group who recorded 'Till The End Of The Day', because here they've issued a humorous, jogging, Joe-Brown-type, semi-comedy number.
Melody Maker, February 1966

I've been mad about folk songs for years and I kept on at Ray to record some. One day I went round to his place and he said 'I've got this idea for a song. It's not a folk song, but more like George Formby.' We both think Formby was brilliant in a social way and that's how Ray got the idea – from listening to George Formby records.
Dave Davies, 1966

Throughout the band's career The Kinks have refused to be manipulated, dictated to by the image-makers, or coerced into being passive mouthpieces.

Those people (managers) told me in their transatlantic accents 'You can't be a pop singer with a gap in your teeth'. They sent me to a bloke to have it fixed up. And just as he was going to do it, I said 'No'. It's the most important decision I've ever made.

Ray Davies, *Melody Maker,* 1971

The distaste for aspects of the corporate music business were most evident in the album 'Lola Versus Powerman And The Money-Go-Round, Part One', with its indictment of the greed of Denmark Street's tin pan alley agents and managers.

Raymond Douglas Davies, King Kong man, taking a cheeky nibble at capitalism and the hurdy-hurdy pop playground. You can't beat the man's hilarity, spiked with cunning.
Melody Maker, 1970

In this business I've constantly run into corporate figures who want to control and run everything. And to a large extent they do, unfortunately. But in a big way, they are wrong. They can't put the pen in my hand. No one can force me to write what he wants.
Ray Davies, *Trouser Press, 1976*

INFLUENCES

The Kinks original manifestation was as R&B band The Ravens. R&B was their most prominent influence in their original sound mix.

Our influences were people like Big Bill Broonzy, Bo Diddley and Chuck Berry, who strangely enough, was not particularly trendy at that time.
Dave Davies, 1978

It was the first genuine British R&B song to be Number 1. We weren't rated as an R&B band although that's where our roots were.
Ray Davies, *Mojo,* 1994

When it comes down to it, the answer is no one record changed my life. It all did.
Ray Davies, *Q* magazine, 1995

*The music of The Kinks touched
a raft of subsequent artists.*

I heard it when I was at school and it really
blew me away; I'd never heard a riff like it. It's
still one of the greatest guitar riffs of all time.

Genesis guitarist **Mike Rutherford,**
on 'You Really Got Me', Q magazine, 1995

We drove a hundred miles to see The Kinks
when I was 18 or something. After the show my
girlfriend and I hung around . . . . And then they
came out, and as he walked by me Ray Davies
dropped his towel where I was sitting. And he
bent over and picked it up and he looked at me,
and I looked at him, and he said hello.

Chrissie Hynde on her first encounter with Ray Davies – years
later The Pretenders recorded The Kinks's 'Stop Your Sobbing'
and she and Davies were a couple for some years

Without them, the music of the Small Faces,
David Bowie, the Sex Pistols, Billy Bragg, Elvis
Costello, Madness, Blur and many others
including ourselves, would not be the same.

Chris Difford and **Glenn Tilbrook** of Squeeze, on The Kinks, 1995

Of the next generation of songwriters, Paul Weller was openly an admirer. In particular, The Jam released a cover of Davies's 'David Watts' from their 'All Mod Cons' album in 1978.

'David Watts' was an obscure Kinks tune, but Ray Davies's teenage hero-worship lyric fitted the Jam like a glove.

Critic **Nigel Cross**

Like Ray Davies of The Kinks, Paul Weller is obsessed with England . . . . On 'Setting Sons' he takes a broader sweep all round.

Record Mirror

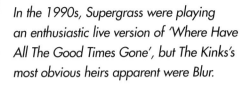

*In the 1990s, Supergrass were playing
an enthusiastic live version of 'Where Have
All The Good Times Gone', but The Kinks's
most obvious heirs apparent were Blur.*

I was in love with him for that hour.
Blur's **Damon Albarn** on Ray Davies
after appearing with him on 'The White
Room', and duetting on 'Waterloo Sunset'
and 'Parklife'.

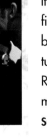

Someone pointed out to me that when he's
playing the piano, Damon's not looking at Ray.
It's as if he's so in awe of Ray Davies that he
can't look at him and play at the same time.
Chris Cowey, producer of 'The
White Room', Q magazine, 1995

It's very funny with people like Blur. I
find it difficult to find my own footprints
because their feet are in 'em. Damon
turns up doing 'Waterloo Sunset' with
Ray Davies – it's me! There's only so
much space for all these influences.
Suggs, of Madness, *NME*

MUSICAL MOMENTS

*The Kinks's early chart toppers were songs
of lusty loneliness, draped behind the
crunching chords of 'You Really Got Me'
and 'All Day And All Of The Night'.*

'You Really Got Me' as a record was a different
record for that time, there was nothing around like it.
I remember I used to go down to the Marquee and
everyone was close to making a record like that. The
Yardbirds thought they'd do it, but we did it first.

Ray Davies

It wasn't really pop or rock'n'roll like they knew it.
And I suppose it came about by accident anyway,
sittin' in me front room, bored.

Dave Davies, *Trouser Press,* 1978

I just knew I had a great song. I didn't want to write
another song after that, oddly enough. Remember,
Dave was 16 years old. It's some feat that record.
Simplistic as hell but so dynamic.

Ray Davies

There was a direct route from the power rock of singles like 'All Day And All Of The Night' to heavy rock, metal and punk.

I think 'All Day' is one of my favourites because of the chord changes, that type of thing hadn't been done before.
Ray Davies

Our latest record is a sincere effort to convey the attitude of many people today.
Ray Davies, 1964

It was the start of heavy metal and it can still stand up against any record by Metallica or Megadeth.
Ray Davies, *Mojo,* 1995

Out of the singles condensing personality types into three-minute thumb-nail sketches, 1968's '(The Kinks Are) The Village Green Preservation Society' and 1969's 'Arthur (Or The Decline And Fall Of The British Empire)' marked the start of a string of concept albums.

Hey, punk . . . . Quit chewing on that razor blade and dip into your history book. Just think of The Kinks and the pure trashy glory of 'Beautiful Delilah', 'You Really Got Me' and 'All Day And All Of The Night'. This was before Ray Davies (*The* Face of the Sixties, for anyone with a soupcon of discernment) threw himself prostrate before the Great God Concept, a rash act which produced several gems but also a great deal of dreck as it took Davies dangerously nearer to the Celine than The Standells.

Julie Burchill, *NME, 1977*

'Lola' was a much needed hit in 1970, at a time when the concept albums were threatening to overpower the sheer commerciality of Ray Davies's earlier, less grandiose, writing.

I had a couple of months when I had to do something else, when I wasn't thinking of music, and it was the first song I wrote after the break. The only thing I had to think about was the beginning, getting the thing to sell in the first five seconds. The rest came naturally. Or unnaturally.

Ray Davies, *NME, 1977*

Circus: Did you know that 'Lola' is the Gay Liberation's song? It's their anthem.

Ray: No, but I had a suspicion it might be. That's nice. 'Lola' is several people really. I tried to analyze it because I do think she's several people. Suppressed love.

Circus magazine, 1974

MoDERN iCoNS ●-THE KINKS

Despite the ups and downs, the retirements and returns, The Kinks live on – their 1993 album 'Phobia' contains the song 'Hatred (A Duet)', a reference to the turbulence at the heart of the Davies brothers' complex relationship.

Circus: Could the Kinks go on without you?

Ray: Yeah.

Circus: When do you think you'll quit?

Ray: I thought about it this morning. I think about it every morning, you know, until I get up and start playing music and I get interested in it again.

Circus magazine, 1974

THE MUSIC

★★★★★   **Essential listening**
★★★   **OK**
★   **Frankly, not the best!**

SINGLES

Long Tall Sally/I Took My Baby Home – February 1964 ★★★

You Really Got Me/It's Alright – August 1964 ★★★★★

All Day And All Of The Night/I Gotta Move – October 1964 ★★★★1/2

Dedicated Follower Of Fashion/Sitting On My Sofa – February 1966 ★★★★★

A Well Respected Man/Milk Cow Blues – April 1966 ★★★★

Sunny Afternoon/I'm Not Like Everybody Else – June 1966 ★★★★★

Dead End Street/Big Black Smoke – November 1966 ★★★★

Waterloo Sunset/Act Nice And Gentle – May 1967 ★★★★★

Autumn Almanac/Mr Pleasant – October 1967 ★★★1/2

Days/B-side – July 1968 ★★★★

Lola/Berkeley Mews – June 1970 ★★★★

Apeman/Rats – November 1970 ★★★1/2

Come Dancing/Noise – July 1983 ★★★

ALBUMS

The Kinks – October 1964 ★★★
Beautiful Delilah/So Mystifying/Just Can't Go To Sleep/Long Tall Shorty/Took My Baby Home/I'm A Lover Not A Fighter/You Really Got Me/Cadillac/Bald Headed Woman/Revenge/Too Much Monkey Business/I've Been Driving On Bald Mountain/Stop Your Sobbing/Got Love If You Want It

The Kink Kontroversy – February 1966 ★★★
Milk Cow Blues/Ring The Bells/Gotta Get The First Plane Home/When I See That Girl Of Mine/I am Free/Till The End Of The Day/The World Keeps Going Round/I'm On An Island/Where Have All The Good Times Gone/It's Too Late/What's In Store For Me/You Can't Win

Face To Face – October 1966 ★★★★1/2
Party Line/Rosy Won't You Please Come Home/Dandy/Too Much On My
Mind/Session Man/Rainy Day In June/House In The Country/Holiday In
Waikiki/Most Exclusive Residence For Sale/Fancy/Little Miss Queen Of
Darkness/You're Looking Fine/Sunny Afternoon/I'll Remember

Something Else By the Kinks – June 1967 ★★★1/2
David Watts/Death Of A Clown/Two Sisters/No Return/Harry Rag/Tin Soldier
Man/Situation Vacant/Love Me Till The Sun Shines/Lazy Old Sun/Afternoon
Tea/Funny Face/End Of The Season/Waterloo Sunset

The Kinks Are The Village Green Preservation Society
– November 1968 ★★★
Village Green Preservation Society/Do You Remember Walter/Picture
Book/Johnny Thunder/The Last Of The Steam Powered Trains/Big Sky/Sitting By
The Riverside/Animal Farm/Village Green/Starstruck/Phenomenal Cat/All My
Friends Were There/Wicked Annabella/Monica/People Take Pictures Of
Each Other

Arthur (Or The Decline And Fall Of The British Empire)
– October 1969 ★★★★
Victoria/Yes Sir, No Sir/Some Mother's Son/Brainwashed/Drivin'/Australia/
Shangri-La/Mr. Churchill Says/She Bought A Hat Like Princess Marina/Young
And Innocent Days/Nothing To Say/Arthur

Part 1: Lola Versus Powerman & The Money-Go-Round
– November 1970 ★★★
The Contenders/Strangers/Denmark Street/Get Back In Line/Lola/Top Of
The Pops/The Moneygoround/This Time Tomorrow/A Long Way From
Home/Rats/Apeman/Powerman/Got To Be Free

Muswell Hillbillies – November 1971 ★★★1/2
20th Century Man/Acute Schizophrenia Paranoia Blues/Holiday/Skin And
Bone/Alcohol/Complicated Life/Here Come The People In Grey/Have A
Cuppa Tea/Holloway Jail/Oklahoma U.S.A./Uncle Sun/Muswell Hillbillies

Schoolboys In Disgrace – November 1975 ★★1/2
Schooldays/Jack The Idiot Dunce/Education/The First Time We Fall In Love/
I'm In Disgrace/Headmaster/The Hard Way/The Last Assembly/No More
Looking Back/Finale

Sleepwalker – February 1977 ★★★1/2
Life On The Road/Mr Big Man/Sleepwalker/Brother/Juke Box Music/Sleepless
Night/Stormy Sky/Full Moon/Life Goes On

Misfits – May 1978 ★★1/2
Misfits/Hay Fever/Live Life/A Rock'n'Roll Fantasy/In A Foreign Land/Permanent
Waves/Black Messiah/Out Of The Wardrobe/Trust Your Heart/Get Up

State Of Confusion – June 1983 ★★★
State Of Confusion/Definite Maybe/Labour Of Love/Come
Dancing/Property/Don't Forget To Dance/Young Conservatives/Heart Of
Gold/Cliches Of The World (B Movie)/Bernadette

THE HISTORY

September 1963
R&B band The Ravens, quartet including Ray and Dave Davies, bassist Pete
Quaife and drummer John Stuart are picked up by businessmen Robert
Wace and Grenville Collins.

November 1963
The Ravens are renamed The Kinks. Mick Avory comes in as drummer.

December 1963
First appearance as The Kinks at the Lotus House restaurant.

February 1964
Having signed to Pye Records, debut single 'Long Tall Sally' released.

September 1964
Third single 'You Really Got Me' goes to Number 1 in the UK.

October 1964
Debut album 'Kinks' released.

January 1965
After a tour of Australia, The Kinks stop off in New York to appear on the TV show 'Hullabaloo'. The hosts are disturbed when Ray and Dave dance together on screen.

May 1965
The group have to pull out of tour with The Yardbirds and others after an on-stage fight between Avory and Dave Davies ends with latter getting head injuries.

June 1965
Live US debut in New York. A fight between Ray Davies and a Musicians Union official gets The Kinks blacklisted in the States for four years.

February 1966
'Dedicated Follower Of Fashion' released – Ray's new songwriting direction emerges.

July 1966
'Sunny Afternoon' goes to Number 1 – England win the World Cup!

September 1966
Quaife leaves band temporarily, replaced by John Dalton, who takes over permanently when Quaife decides not to re-join.

December 1966
Quaife rejoins! Finally leaves in 1969, to be replaced permanently by John Dalton.

August 1967
Dave Davies issues solo single 'Death Of A Clown' which gets to Number 3.

October 1967
'Something Else', the first Kinks album produced by Ray Davies, reaches Number 35 – the last original Kinks album to chart in the UK.

November 1968
'The Kinks Are The Village Green Preservation Society' released.

October 1969
'Arthur (Or The Decline And Fall Of The British Empire)' released; originally commissioned as a TV play, only the album saw the light of day.

June 1970
Ray Davies has to make a 6,000 mile round trip from New York to London and back to re-record two words on 'Lola': 'Coca-Cola' is changed to 'cherry cola', the single later charts at Number 2. John Gosling, who plays keyboards on 'Lola' joins permanently in 1971.

July 1973
During a show at the White City Stadium, London, Ray announces he is leaving the music business for good (his wife had walked out on him the previous month), but he is back a week later. Dave Davies drops out of the group for a couple of years, though.

July 1977
Dave Davies is back on side again, and
'Sleepwalker' gets to 21 in the US, where
The Kinks have a strong following.

March 1978
John Dalton leaves definitively (having been
'temporarily' replace by Andy Pyle for two years),
as does Gosling. They are replaced by ex-Argent
bassist Jim Rodford, and Gordon Edwards on
keyboards.

February 1979
The Pretenders release Ray Davies's 'Stop Your
Sobbing' – singer Chrissie Hynde will later
become romantically involved with Davies, before
leaving him for Jim Kerr of Simple Minds in 1984.

July 1979
Ian Gibbons replaces Edwards on keyboards.

July 1983
Long awaited UK and US hit with 'Come Dancing'.

April 1986
Ray Davies plays Patsy Kensit (Crepe Suzette)'s father in Julien Temple's film
'Absolute Beginners'.

January 1990
The Kinks are inducted into the Rock and Roll Hall of Fame. Three
months later they receive a Special Contribution To British Music
award at the Ivor Novello awards.

September 1994
Ray Davies's autobiography *X-Ray* published –
becomes the basis of a touring one-man show.

THE CAST

Mick Avory. Born 15 February 1944, Hampton, Surrey. Joins The Ravens/Kinks in answer to an ad placed by Dave Davies in Melody Maker. After leaving in 1984, replaced by Bob Henrit. Plays with a number of other bands, and occasionally with John Dalton's Kast Off Kinks.

John Dalton. Originally stands in for Pete Quaife on bass in 1966 when Quaife is injured in a road accident; has previously played in The Mark Four and Creation. When Quaife finally leaves for good in 1969, Dalton joins permanently, departing in 1976. Later fronts the Kast Off Kinks, an occasional Kinks tribute band.

Dave Davies. Born 3 February 1947, Muswell Hill, London. Releases successful Top 3 solo single 'Death Of A Clown' in 1967. Leaves The Kinks temporarily in the mid-Seventies. In later Kinks days gets into soundtrack composition, including two John Carpenter movies.

Ray Davies. Born 21 June 1944, Muswell Hill, London. An art school student, joins Dave's school band. 'Leaves' The Kinks on numerous occasions, most notoriously in 1973 while supporting the Edgar Broughton Band at London's White City Stadium. Takes over management of the band in 1971. Emerges as grand old man of rock, releases autobiography *X-Ray* in 1994, and enjoys solo glory.

Other Kinks: Keyboard player John Gosling joins in 1970 from his course at the Royal Academy, quits 1978. Andy Pyle (ex-Blodwyn Pig and the Alvin Lee Band) takes over bass duties from John Dalton between 1976 and 1978 – after leaving, puts together short-lived band United with Gosling. Gosling and Pyle replaced respectively by Gordon Edwards (ex-Pretty Things) and John Rodford (ex-Argent) in 1978. Further variations ensue.

Peter Quaife. Born 31 December 1943, Tavistock, Devon. Meets Dave Davies at secondary school, and joins his band. Following a somewhat protracted decision to leave the band in 1969, he moves to Copenhagen with his Danish wife, working as a freelance illustrator, eventually emigrating to Canada.

Shel Talmy. Born 1940, Chicago. Comes to the UK and becomes the first independent producer, working for Decca with The Bachelors. Is The Kinks's producer for a fruitful four years, and produces The Who, including 'My Generation'. Also works with Manfred Mann, Amen Corner, Pentangle and String Driven Thing, and The Damned, before returning to the States.

THE BOOKS

Kink: An Autobiography – Dave Davies (Boxtree) 1996
The Kinks: Well Respected Men – Neville Marten &
        Jeffrey Hudson (Castle Communications) 1996
X-Ray – Ray Davies (Penguin) 1994

PICTURE CREDITS

Pages 2-3 Gems/Redferns. **Page 5** David Redfern/Redferns. **Page 8** LFI. **Page 10** David Redfern/Redferns. **Page 13** Colin Fuller/Redferns. **Page 14** LFI. **Page 15** LFI. **Page 16** David Redfern/Redferns. **Page 17** Nick Elgar/LFI. **Page 18** Redferns. **Page 19** Steve Gillett/Redferns. **Page 20** Steve Morley/ Redferns. **Page 21** Gems/Redferns. **Pages 22-3** (l) Fryderyk Gabowicz/ Redferns; (r) LFI. **Page 24** Richie Aaron/Redferns. **Page 25** LFI. **Page 26** David Redfern/Redferns. **Pages 26-7** LFI. **Pages 28-9** Val Wilmer/ Redferns. **Pages 30-1** (l) LFI; (r) David Redfern/Redferns. **Pages 32-3** (l) David Redfern/ Redferns; (r) David Redfern/Redferns. **Page 34** LFI. **Page 35** LFI. **Pages 36-7** LFI. **Page 38** Erica Echenberg/Redferns. **Page 39** LFI **Page 40** Petra Niemeier/Redferns. **Page 41** Petra Niemeier/Redferns. **Pages 42-3** (t) Paul Cox/LFI; (b) Ian Dickson/Redferns. **Page 44** Ian Dickson/Redferns. **Page 45** Dave Ellis/Redferns. **Page 47** Steve Gillett/ Redferns. **Page 48** Des Willie/Redferns. **Page 49** Des Willie/Redferns. **Pages 50-1** Nick Elgar/ LFI. **Pages 52-3** (l) LFI; (r) Steve Morley/Redferns. **Page 55** Paul Cox/LFI. **Page 56** LFI. **Pages 58-9** Kevin Mazur/LFI. **Pages 60-1** Petra Neimeier/Redferns. **Pages 62-3** LFI. **Pages 64-5** Gems/Redferns. **Page 66** Ian Dickson/Redferns. **Pages 66-7** Erica Echenberg/Redferns. **Pages 68-9** (t) LFI; (b) David Redfern/Redferns. **Page 70** Patrick Ford/Redferns. **Page 73** Steve Morley/Redferns. **Page 74** Des Willie/Redferns. **Page 75** Des Willie/ Redferns. **Pages 76-7** Redferns. **Pages 78-9** Lorne Resnick/Redferns. **Page 80** (t) LFI; (b) Colin Fuller/Redferns. **Pages 82-3** Erica Echenberg/Redferns. **Page 85** Gems/Redferns. **Page 86** Dave Ellis/Redferns. **Page 89** David Redfern/Redferns. **Page 90** David Redfern/Redferns. **Page 91** Des Willie/Redferns.